NOW

1) IN BLOOM
2) SEGWAY
3) DESTINATION

A LIFE LIVED. LISTED OUT IN THREE STEPS. LIVE A LIFE WORTH WRITING ABOUT AFTER THE BOOK. NOW, AND BE EVER-CHANGING.

IN BLOOM

SELF SAME

CREATION IS OUR GIFT
DESTRUCTION OUR ASPIRATION
SELF SAME POSTURE TAMED
TRAVEL AND POUND EARTH

RECITE YOUR LINES
SNIFF THEM IF YOU MUST
SMELLING ROSES IS FOR THE YOUNG
WE ARE CHAMPIONS HERE

RIDE FAST TRAVEL SLOW
SHOW THEM ALL YOU BEAT IT OUT
LET YOUR HEART BE THE BELL
AND KID, GIVE 'EM HELL

THE UNDENIABLE, INSUFFERABLE URGE TO BE DIFFERENT. THE DESIRE TO LEAVE ONE'S MARK ON SOCIETY. MY DRIVE TO BE IN A HISTORY BOOK. OUR DRIVE TO BE IN A HISTORY BOOK. TAKE IT ALL WITH YOU WHEN YOU GO. UNLIVE THE GENERATIONS BEFORE YOU. DENY HISTORICAL PRESETS THE JOY THEY GET WHEN YOU DIE ALONE, POOR AND UNRECOGNIZED. SHIP AN EAR TO A WOMAN WHO NOTICED HOW PERFECTLY YOUR EARS FIT YOUR FACE. LIVE A LIFE UNNECESSARY TO THE PAST, SO THE FUTURE CAN LIVE. BY ANY MEANS. BY ANY MEANS THAT YOU NEED. JUSTIFY YOUR PATH BASED ONLY UPON YOUR OPINION OF YOU. NEVER BE THE SAME SELF TWICE.

FLOWER

THE FLOWER WAS BEAUTIFUL
BEFORE YOU ARRIVED
YOU PLUCKED HER FROM THE GARDEN
ON YOUR OWN NEEDS
SHE WENT WITH
HELPLESS AND CAPTIVE
SHE DIED THAT WAY
FOR YOU
THE FLOWER WAS BORN
JUST TO DIE
BUT LET HER DIE FREE
AND FULL OF ART

THE SPIDER IS A THIRD PARTY
EMBODIMENT
TRAPPED THE FLY
AND SUCKED HIM DRY
SPIDER NEVER CARED
FOR THE DEMANDS OF FLOWER
FLOWER NEVER MEANT
FOR YOU TO GET KILLED
FLY WAS HARVESTED
FOR ITS DEATH MEAT
KEEP OUT OF THE WEBS
AND FLY FREE

A MAN LOVED A WOMEN ONCE, A MILLION TIMES, SPANNED ACROSS MANY GENERATIONS. SHE NEVER MEANT FOR HIM TO GET KILLED. HE NEVER MEANT TO REMOVE HER FROM WHAT MADE HER BEAUTIFUL. THE FLY TRIED TO GIVE THE FLOWER WHAT HE BELIEVED TO BE SOMETHING SHE COULD NEED. SHE NEEDS NOT A THING. THE SPIDER SLEPT NEARBY THE BEAUTIFUL FLOWER AND STARTED THE JOURNEY ALL OVER. REINCARNATION'S EDIT OF HELL FOR THE TWO ROMANTICS. AND A BLOOD THIRSTY FIEND.

DES MOINES RIVER

ONE NIGHT DOWN BY
THE DES MOINES RIVER
YOU ASKED IF I EVER
DATED HER AND I SAID YES
THAT TIME I VISITED YOU
IN THE CAROLINAS
HER AND I DATED
FOR A YEAR AND A HALF THEN

YOU ASKED IF I EVER
KISSED HER, I COULDN'T LIE
THEN YOU WANTED TO KNOW
IF YOU MET HER
I SAID NO, I DIDN'T WANT TO
BURDEN YOU WITH THAT
YOU SAW MY EYES AND WANTED
ME TO RETURN TO HER FOREVER

AS MY DAUGHTER AGES.
RELATIONSHIPS AND OTHER
ADULTHOODS BECOME HER
FASCINATIONS. SHE WANTS,
AS I DO FOR HER, ONLY THE
BEST AND HAPPINESS. THE
FLY AND THE FLOWER CAN
NEVER BALANCE IN
HARMONY. AND I WISH SHE
NEVER HAS TO LEARN HOW
AND WHY. LIFE IN THE POEMS
SPILLS OVER UNTO PEOPLE
THAT SHOULDN'T FEEL THE
RADIOACTIVITY OF A LIFE
ONCE LIVED. THE STORIES
AND SCARS WE CARRY WITH
US SPILL OUT ONTO A
CANVAS FOR
CONVERSATION'S SAKE. AND
I, THE HOPELESS ROMANTIC,
TRAVELS ON.

WATER WITH DISPARITIES

WATER IN A WELL SO COLD AND WITHDRAWN
HIDDEN FROM EYES OF MISCHIEF AND DECEIT
THEY SEEK TO CONSUME OF YOUR WATER
THEY CARE NOT HOW THEY RETURN YOU TO EARTH

THE WATER OF LIFE LIVES ON ITS OWN
TO BE BURIED BY ITS LOVING CREATOR
NOT AS PUNISHMENT BUT PROTECTION
TO HIDE WATER FROM THE CONSUMER

IN DEATH METAMORPHOSIS MENDED
A MENAGERIE OF BROKEN DREAMS
ADVENTURES LOSS THE OCEAN AFAR
TO GROW UP EXTRA LARGE AND SALTY

A RIVER FLOWS WILD AND RUSHES WITH RAGE
THE TIDE FIGHTS BACK AGAINST THEM
THOSE WHO DESIRE TO CONSUME WATER
RETURN YOU TO EARTH WITH EXISTING DISPARITIES

THE BODILY DEATH IS NOT TO BE FEARED. THE JOURNEY OF YOUR SOUL IS THE TRUEST IMPORTANCE FOR US. WEATHER A SOUL SUCKER, BUILDS A TAP AND ATTEMPTS TO TAKE YOUR WATER AND WHAT MAKES YOU BEAUTIFULLY AND IMPERFECTLY YOU. DON'T LET THEM CHANGE YOU. OCEANS OF WATER AND HEAVENS OF SOULS IN ONE GRAND METAPHOR FOR SALVATION. FIGHT LIKE THE MIGHTIEST RIVER TO MAKE IT HOME TO THE OCEAN OR THE KINGDOM OF GOLD PROMISED BY GOD, YOUR CREATOR.

BRUSHES

THE LITTLE THINGS LIKE
A PAINT BRUSH IN HER TOOTHBRUSH CUP
SHE HAS BRUSHES CAN TRAVEL,
SHE HAS HER GOALS IN ORDER
PAINTBRUSH, TOOTHBRUSH,
AND A HAIR BRUSH ON THE SIDE
ALL OF EQUAL IMPORTANCE
FOR GOOD SUSTAINABLE LIVING

THE YEAR MY DAUGHTER HAD HER OWN BATHROOM AT MY HOUSE. WAS THE SAME SUMMER THAT HOUSE BECAME A HOME AGAIN. THIS WRITING BRINGS ME SUCH A SINCERE SMILE. I WANDERED IN TO CHECK ON THINGS AND CLEAN UP A BIT AS I WALKED PAST ON THE COUNTER NEXT TO HER SINK. THE STRATEGIC MOVE TO DRY HER PAINT BRUSHES IN HER TOOTHBRUSH CUP. HOW INCREDIBLE AND HOW INTELLIGENT. THEY ARE THE SAME THING, ART IS ART IS ART IS ART.

BIG

I WAS A FEW TOWNS OVER FILLING MY TRUNK
YOU CLEARED A HOUSE WITH JUST ANOTHER MAN
YOUR BIG BROTHER TAUGHT US SO MUCH
I WISH I WOULD'VE HEARD YOUR HALF WITH YOU

HE SAID TO ALWAYS DEFEND YOUR FAMILY
STAND UP TALL AND DON'T SHY FROM A FIGHT
CARRY YOUR OWN WEIGHT WITH YOUR CHEST OUT
STRANGLE A MAN SO HE CAN'T RUN AWAY

I HEARD ALL THE HUSTLING AND MONEY THINGS
DO WRONG IF YOU STAY ONE STEP AHEAD
KEEP RUNNING AND NEVER SLOW DOWN
MAKE MY OWN WAY NO MATTER HOW

NOW WE'RE BIG AND NO ROLE MODELS REMAIN
LITTLE PEOPLE LOOKING UP AT US
I STILL WISH I WAS TEACHING THEM YOUR HALF
INSTEAD OF WATCHING THEM SLIP AWAY

WHAT A DISTINCT MOMENT WHEN CHILDHOOD STOPS BEING SO INNOCENT AND REALLY STARTED BEING AN ADULT OF THIS SPECIES CALLED HUMAN. HINDSIGHT BEING 20/20 I'M A BIT MORE 10 OUT OF 10 IN MY MEMORIES AND SO ARE THE ONES I LOVE. I CAN PAINT SOMEONE AS MOTHER THERESA POSING FOR THE MONA LISA IF I LIKE THEIR MEMORIES WELL ENOUGH. NOSTALGIA IS A TERRIBLE LANE TO PARK ON FOR TOO LONG. BUT THIS ONE WAS NEEDED TO SETTLE A FEW HAUNTS.

VELVET

VELVET COVERED HORSES
SANG LULLABY'S FROM THE HEART
GRASSLANDS WORE THEIR ARMOR
SAFE UNDER THEIR REIGN

CLOUDS CRIED UPON THEIR DEPARTURE
THE MAJESTIC CREATURES CHOSE
TO HOLD THE PRAIRIE NEAR
AS THE LAND LOVED THE WOLVES

VELVET IS AN ANALOGY. IT'S AN INARGUABLE PLEASANT AND SOFT TO THE TOUCH PRODUCT. IT IS A CONSTANT UPON WHICH TO MEASURE THE EVIL DEPICTED IN THIS VERBAL PAINTING. IMAGINE EVEN VELVET BEING HATED. THE EVIL OF SOME ITEM WILLING TO BE SO SOFT AND SO PLEASANT JUST FOR THE SAKE OF YOUR ENJOYMENT. THEN HATE IT AND CHOOSE THE CANINE OF A WOLF AS IT CLOSES DOWN UPON YOUR THROAT. YOUR HANDS CALOUS AND DECAY. JOINTS LOSE THEIR FLUIDITY AND YOU SAY YOU LOVE THE POINT OF THE CANINE AND THE BREATH SCENTED OF DEATH AND DECAY.

REQUEST

TELEKINETIC REQUEST
SENT DOWN FROM MY SPINE
A LOVE LETTER BOUND FROM YOURS TO MINE
THIS SIGNAL DAMPENS
THE AIR TO STOP TIME
A CHANNEL KNOWN FROM A BIRTH RIGHT

THE STATIC AIR CLEANSE OUR PALLET
OF PURPLE THE LOSS OF SIN
BECOMES SENSATIONAL
LONGER AND BROADER THE SIGNAL
SEEKS HOME AMONGST YOUR DREAMS
AND OUR PAST LOSSES

MAYBE TOMORROW OUR SIGNAL
WILL CONNECT MAKE CONTACT
TOGETHER LIKE A MARS ATTACK
ASSAULT ON MY HEART
AND WOUNDS RUN DEEP SEEP INTO MY LUNGS
MY VEINS BURST I BLEED OUT

LET ME HOLD YOU THROUGH THE NIGHT
AND FEEL YOUR WARMTH INSIDE
AS I LEARN TO LOVE YOU NOW
AS I LEARN TO LOVE YOU NOW
LEARN TO LOVE YOU
NOW

LOVE IS DEFINED IN OUR EARLIEST YEARS, IT APPEARS FOR MOST OF US. THE STANDARD BY WHAT WE CALL LOVE VERSUS ABUSE HAPPENS SO QUICKLY. WE SPEND EMPTY SORROWFUL EVENINGS TRYING TO DETERMINE WHAT THE REMAINING MOMENTS ARE THERE FOR. WHY WE CALL OUT AND FOLLOW A CERTAIN TASTE OR SCENT AND CAN'T RE WIRE OR EDIT THAT SETTING IN OUR HEARTS. WHY OUR BRAIN CAN'T ARGUE AND WIN AGAINT SUCH A SIMPLE VALVE SYSTEM ORGAN. ALL THE GREY MATTER IN THE WORLD WON'T SAVE YOU FROM A HEART WITH A PLAN.

FEEL

ESCAPE YOUR RESTRAINTS
BACK AWAY FROM FUTURES
LIVE FOR THE NOW
BURN FROM BOTH ENDS

LACK OF FEELING
FLUTTER FORENSICS
ALTERNATE ANTIDOTE
MEDITATE AWAIT

ROBOT TEST DENIED
FINGERPRINTS AND FACES
KEEP THE YOU ON EARTH
WATER REVIVAL

BACK TO THE WATER AND THE SOUL METAPHOR THAT APPEARS OFTEN IN MY BLINDEST WRITINGS. THE ONES I REMEMBER READING AS THOUGH I AM YOU. THESE WRITING MEAN SO MUCH. THEY ARE MESSAGES NOT FROM ME BUT FOR ME. YOU DO HAVE FINGERPRINTS, YOU DO ADAPT, YOU TO HAVE FREE WILL. YOU FEEL. YOU THINK. THERE FOR I AM. BY ANY MEANS.

BLOODBATH

THE BIRTH OF A BLOODBATH
THIS THING OF OURS
IS ALL HAPPENING
THE DEMISE OF WEEK MINDS
THOSE MEANT TO HANG
RARELY GET SHOT, RARELY GET SHOT

NOW TODAY I'M BOUGHT AND SOLD
IF YOU FEEL THE FREEDOM FLOW
THEN SING IT OUT LIKE WE DO
MAKE YOUR SONG HEARD TODAY

FOR THE SHADOWS OF THE FOREST
THE BOY A FALLING TREE FAR FROM SIGHT
UNTIL THE CRASH WAS HEARD
NO ONE KNEW HIS NAME

MY MIND IS FADING EACH DAY
I GET TO CONCENTRATE ON THE NUMB
NEVER TO ATTAIN LIFE UNTIL DUMB
SUBDUE SUBMIT SUBSIDE

BLOODBATH. MY BLACK AND CHROME SQUIER MUSTANG. I'VE ALWAYS WANTED ONE OF THESE. BRITTANY GOT ME ONE FOR CHRISTMAS, THIS ACT OF KINDNESS MEANS MORE THAN THE WORLD. THE POEM OF THE SAME NAME IS A BATTLE CRY, A MISSION STATEMENT. THE UPDATED 10FOUR10 (FROM ART WITH WORDS). STAND UP, IF YOU FEEL THE FREEDOM FLOW. LET YOU BE KNOWN. YOU ARE I AND NOT US. LIVE OUT THE ROGUE LIFE IF YOU'RE GOING TO DIE ALONE ANY WAY. COVERED IN BLOOD THAT'S NOT ONLY YOURS.

GAME

UNCONTESTED YOU ARE THE CHAMP
WITHOUT PEASANTS WHOSE THE KING
ALONE YOU ARE THE FIRST PLACE
AND EACH ENDING THE LAST

TOGETHER IS COMPELLING COMPETITION
APART IS DIFFICULT DESOLATION
TODAY YOU LIVE WITH EARNEST AMBITION
APATHY APART FROM ITSELF IS ANARCHY

ARE YOU SURE THIS IS A GOOD IDEA
WHAT IS TO BE WILL BE ALIVE OR DEAD
WORSE THINGS ACCRUE EVERY HOUR
GREATER GOODS EXIST ALL AROUND

THE FIGHT FOR LOVE. THE BATTLE FOR SUCCESS. THE WAR OUT OF POVERTY. OTHERS DENY. AND LIFE CONTINUES. NO ONE SHOULD BE COMPARED BY ANY ACCOMPLISHMENTS ASIDE FROM AGAINST THEIR OWN. THOSE WHO SETTLE FOR LISTENING AND NEVER TRY TO RELATE ARE YOUR TRUEST FRIENDS AND LOVERS. THE ALMIGHTY I AM WILL DETERMINE NOT YOUR DEATH BUT YOUR LEGACY. THIS LIFE CALLED GAME IS NOT A JOKE, UNTIL YOU MAKE IT. A WISE MAN TOLD ME YOU'RE EITHER FUNNY OR COOL. IF YOU THINK YOU'RE BOTH, IT'S DELUSION.

BROKEN SOUNDS, JOYFUL DREAMS

IMAGINE STOPPING THE GENERATIONAL DEBT OF US
A LITTLE YOU AND A LITTLE ME EXISTING EVERY LIFE TIME
WE COULD BE ADAM AND EVE IT GOES ON THAT LONG
AGAIN YOU ATE THE APPLE, I ATE YOUR EVERY WORD

THIS TIME WE DIDN'T RUIN EVERYTHING ON EARTH
WE FOUND EACH OTHER EVERY 75 YEARS
DERIVATIVE FROM THE BEGINNING OF TIME
TOGETHER WE TAKE OVER, INHERIT THE KINGDOM

CAST SATAN FROM THE CLUTCHES OF SOCIETY
FREE THE WORLD WITH OUR SUCCESS OVER STRIFE
MAKE IT LOOK SO EASY WITH THE WORLD ON OUR BACK
NOTHING CLICHE, NO ONE COULD EXPLAIN OUR EUPHORIA

IMAGINE STOPPING THE GENERATIONAL DEBT OF US
IMAGINE SURVIVING THE LOSS OF A SOUL TIME AND AGAIN
IMAGINE A SOUL DESIGNED FOR MY COMPLETION
IMAGINE THE SALVATION OF HUMANITY THROUGH
ADAM AND EVE

LOVE, A MILLION ATTEMPTS FOR LOVE. ACROSS GENERATIONS, MILLENNIA, THROUGH NATIONS, OVER OCEANS, LOVE. A STORY FOR EVERYTHING, AS THOUGH IT'S BEEN LIVED DAY IN AND DAY OUT. THE TIMELINE OF A DOZEN MOONS CAN'T EXPLAIN THE KNOWLEDGE INHERITED FROM LOVE THAT FAILS SINCE THE FIRST AFFAIR OF ADAM AND EVE.

BROKEN WING

IT'S TIME TO FLY FREE AND SING
LITTLE BIRD WITH THE BROKEN WING
BROWN BIRD GOT CAUGHT IN A SNARE
BOUND AND NOW MENDED AWARE

THE BINDS THAT HEAL
NOW BEGIN TO STEAL
DEATH IS YOUR FREEDOM
STOCKHOLM SYNDROME

A POEM OF
AUTOBIOGRAPHICAL DEPTH.
IF ONLY THIS ONE WAS
ABOUT SOMEONE ELSE, I
COULD JUST WALK HOME. THE
EXIT STRATEGY OF
CHILDHOOD IS PAIN. IT MAKES
US ADULTS. THICKENS THE
SKIN AND PREPARES US FOR
LIFE ALONE. GIVES A MAN A
VOICE THE LIKES OF WAYLON
OR THOSE LADIES IN
SHAWSHANK REDEMPTION.
WE ENVY AND CHERISH THEIR
AWE AND WONDER. THOUGH,
WOULD NEVER
INTELLIGENTLY TRADE THE
LIFE THAT MAKES A VOICE
LIKE THAT.

DEVICES IN POVERTY

EVEN THOUGH YOU DON'T HATE ME
YOU ARE ALLOWED TO LOVE ME
A COUNTRY OF MEN LIVING FROM
ONE VIOLENT CLIMAX TO ANOTHER
OUR ONE CERTAIN BOTTOMLESS COMMODITY
SUPPLIES ARE ENDLESS
THE WELL WILL NEVER RUN DRY
AND ALWAYS PROVIDE THIS EXPORT

AND WHY NOT THERE WAS NOTHING
GOOD ON TV ANYWAYS
THE MOTEL GOT CLEANED UP
AND THE RIFF RAFF EVACUATED
ENTERTAINMENT WAS LEFT TO OUR OWN
DEVICES IN POVERTY
FINANCIAL DEFICIT AND CREATIVITY
STEMMED FROM PORNOGRAPHY

NO CONSUMERS LEFT IN A BROKEN CLASS
FORMERLY THE MIDDLE CLASS
BLUE COLLAR AND GOVERNMENT RELIANCE
BUILDS FOR BOREDOM
NO ART WITH A DIET THIS POOR
AND UNNOURISHED TOO BUSY
WE SELF CONSUME AND IMAGINE
NOTHING WHILE SIMULATING LIFE

THE MODERN HUMAN IS VOID OF LIFE, PHYSICAL LIFE. ON THE MAJORITY. AFFLUENCE AND LUXURIES ARE TOO APLENTY FOR THE STRIFE THAT BUILDS A TRADITIONAL HUMAN. A DESCENT LIFE IS DEFINED BY OBSCURE CONSEQUENCES. OUR CONSCIENCE DISSOLVED UNTO SITCOMS AND VULGARITY FOR THE SAKE OF VULGAR WORDS. THEY DON'T GET USED NEAR ENOUGH ANYWAY.

STOP

JUST SO LONG AS IT STOPS
MY BRAIN FROM THINKING
SLOWS OPERATIONS DOWN
AND MINIMIZES INTERACTIONS

THE CONVERSATIONS MUST STOP
BETWEEN MY BRAIN AND MYSELF
THE ART WILL GO WITH IT
SHUT IT DOWN FOR MY SAKE

THIS DYSFUNCTION WILL STOP
I WILL BELONG TO SOCIETY
BLENDED LIKE A MASTERPIECE
MY FINALE PRESENTATION TO EARTH

AN OVER MEDICATED GENERATION. WHERE ARTISTS AND STORYTELLERS ARE SUPPOSED TO HAVE A DEGREE, NOT A LIVED LIFE. EXPERIENCES ARE TOO BE SUBSTITUTED FOR READ KNOWLEDGE. STUDY OTHERS DON'T WRITE YOUR OWN. MEMORIES OF THE SUBLIMINALS OF SOCIETY AND IGNORE YOUR OWN EXAGGERATIONS AND VENTURES. NEVER I, ONLY THEM AND THOSE. TO QUOTE ZACH DAVIDSON. "IF I WERE YOU THEN I WOULD MEMORIZE THIS LOOSE LIPPED LULLABY, INSTEAD OF WAITING, CARVING OUT YOUR OWN."

YEARS AWAY

I MISSED YOU SO BAD FOR ALL THOSE YEARS...

MUST'VE BEEN YOUR WANTING
BLEEDING THROUGH THE WORLD
INTO MY LONELY HEART KEEPING ME
WARM ON THE COLDEST NIGHTS

YEARS AWAY UNTIL A BETTER DAY
GOOD AND BAD IMMEASURABLE
TIME SCALED ACROSS A LIFELINE
YOUR HEART BEATS TO KEEP ME ALIVE

PUMPKIN PATCHES, CHILD LIKE MEMORIES
TREES FOR CELEBRATIONS OF LOST CAUSES
TRADITIONS BLOWN OUT OF OUR WAY
THE LAMB TO THE SLAUGHTER

A TRAGIC MOMENT REVERBERATED INTO AN AWFUL CLIMAX AND RETURNED A LOVE THOUGHT LOST. A POISON WAS CURED. A CHILDHOOD WAS KILLED AND AN INNOCENCE STOLEN, IN THE AFTERMATH A BEAUTIFUL MOMENT RETURNED. LIKE A CHOCOLATE COVERED STRAWBERRY IN A NUCLEAR BLAST. IT'S BEEN SAID "SOME OF GOD'S GREATEST GIFTS ARE UNANSWERED PRAYERS." AFTER I WROTE THIS, I'LL NEVER KNOW IF THAT'S TRUE.

SONG OF THE WORM

THE SIREN SONG OF THE CHILD SOLDIER
CRIES THE BABY BOY BEATEN BY A FATHER
THE CROCODILE TEARS OF A DAUGHTER
STRONGER AND SELF AWARE FOR LIFE

WHEN THAT NEIGHBOR BABYSITS
MOM THINKS IT'S JUST A NIGHT OUT
LITTLE MAN WON'T BE A BOY AGAIN
BLOOD DRAWN AND A HEART SLAUGHTERED

LITTLE GIRL, LITTLE ONE STAND STRONG
ADDICTION CAN'T CURE THIS WOUND
A MIND SPLIT IN TWO FROM AGE SEVEN
CAN'T EVER RELIVE INNOCENCE ENTRANCED

FATHER, FATHER SPARE THE BOYS SKULL
A FIST OF A MAN SHOULD NEVER STRIKE
LIE DOWN AND SLEEP ALONE WORM
NEVER TAKE YOUR DAUGHTER TO BED

WHAT CAUSES THE WEAK AND SELFISH BELIEFS OF A CHILD ABUSER IS NEVER WORTH THE TIME OF A DAY FOR THOSE OF US WITH GOOD HEARTS. MY PARENTS ARE GREAT PEOPLE. I SPEAK UPON ABUSE STRICTLY FROM SECOND HAND OCCASIONS. THE MOMENTS OF WHICH WERE CLOSEST TO MY MIND I WON'T SHARE NAMES FOR THE SAKE OF THE CHILDREN AND THEIR ATTEMPTS TO BECOME BETTER THAN THEIR PREDECESSORS. NOT TO EXCUSE THE WEAK WORMS THAT ACTED ON THEIR OWN SELFISH AND INHUMAN CHOICES. INNOCENCE IS TO BE PROTECTED AND THOSE THAT CHOSE TO DEFILE OUR CHILDREN ARE NOT OF THE SAME BREED NOR SPECIES OF THOSE OF US THAT CARE. IT'S THAT SIMPLE. WELCOME TO THE NEXT STAGE OF LIFE. ENDURE YOUR CONSEQUENCES.

SEGWAY

BROKE

I BROKE OUT
IN SEARCH OF
THE BAD GUY
ALL I FOUND WAS ME

TODAY WAS GREEN
YESTERDAY GOLD
TOMORROW UNKNOWN
THE WORLD TO OWN

CARS FOR DRIVING
WOMEN TO ADORE
OR REVERSE IT BACK
LIVE FOR THE ATTACK

SEGWAY INTO THE NEXT STAGES OF LIFE. GIVE UP THE PAST AND ALL CRUTCHES ENDURED DURING ITS SPAN. THE NEXT CHAPTER OF A LIFE. TRYING TO FIND ROLE MODELS JUST TO NEVER WANT TO MEET THEM AGAIN. FULL OF LIFE, NOTHING GOLD CAN STAY. WOMEN SEEM SO APPEALING BUT BUILDING A RESPECTABLE HOT ROD, THAT DRIVES FAST, CAMS LOUD AND GETS YOU TO THE MIDDLE OF NOWHERE MAY BE A BETTER INVESTMENT OF TIME AND ENERGY. FIND YOURSELF, LOVE YOURSELF AND DATE YOU.

CHEMICAL

CHEMICAL AND LETHAL INJECTION
BY ADDICTION AND FALSEHOODS
YOU HAVE ALL BEEN LIED TO
THIS IS ALL IN YOUR HEAD SHE SAID
GET UP, STAND UP LEAVE THIS
ILLUSIONARY IMPRISONING DREAD
DRIVE AND STRIVE FIND LIFE
DESIRE AND MOTIVATE TO FIND GOODS

SHE LIVES FOR HER OWN WANTS
WHAT SHE CONSIDERS HER DESIRES
THE STANDARDS OF LOW LIFE LIVING
SHOWN TO HER JUST WON'T PROVIDE
LIFE IS MEANT TO MAKE A STATEMENT
HER GOALS DRIVEN TO NEVER HIDE
TOMORROW, TOMORROW WHAT A LIE
PROVIDED TO EXTINGUISH FIRES

THE PREVENTION OF SELF. THE PROGRESSION OF ONENESS. THE GROWTH OF HUMANITY. BEING THE GOOD YOU WANT FROM THIS WORLD IS DISTRACTED AND STOLEN FROM AT EVERY TURN OF THE DAY. IMMEASURABLE TIME BUT A STANDARD NEEDS SET. GOD GAVE US DAY AND NIGHT TO HELP US MEASURE A LIFE. NOT TO BE COMPARED TO ANOTHER. JUST ACCEPT YOU AS YOUR OWN. THE DRUGS WERE NEVER MEANT FOR HUMAN CONSUMPTION. DIET AND EXERCISE BY YOUR OWN BODY'S STANDARDS. LISTEN TO YOUR BRAIN AND BEAT TO YOUR HEART.

SHADOW BOX

A CERAMIC PIG PAINTED UP
TO LOOK SO REAL
LOOK TO CLOSE AND YOU
CAN SEE LUNGS BREATHE
A TWO DOLLAR BILL
GLUED TO THE BACK
LIKE A FLAG, NOW VIEWED
AS A TOMBSTONE

HERE LIES A LIFE
ONCE LIVED IN PASSION
THE PIG ROAMED FREE
AND FEARED, A DAREDEVIL
A TWO DOLLAR BILL
AMERICAN CURRENCY
BOTH FROZEN IN A MOMENT
OF HIGH LIVING

HIGH ON THE HOG
STRUCK DOWN NOW
NO LAST MEAL
JUST A LETHAL VERDICT
CORPORAL PUNISHMENT
WORE A BLINDFOLD
HIDDEN EYES DON'T DESERVE
THIS SWAN SONG

FIGHT YOUR SELF. SHADOW BOX A MIRROR. BUILD A KEEPSAKE OF EVERY MOMENT THAT PRODUCED A RESPONSIVE ACTION FROM YOURSELF THAT YOU APPRECIATE. BURN THOSE MEMORIES BEFORE THEY BECOME YOUR BACKING TRACK SKIPPING ON REPEAT, LIKE A SCRATCHED CD FROM A CRUSH. SCRATCHED WITH RAZOR BLADES. KILL YOUR IDOLS. MELT THE GOLDEN LILLIE. PLUCK THE FLOWER AND RELEASE HER TO THE CROSSWINDS ABOVE. A MIGHTY CREATURE MEANT FOR ADORATION SHOULD NEVER BE HELD BEHIND GLASS. MONEY IS MEANT TO BE SOLD NOT CHERISHED. WE BOTH SINNED, I JUST DIDN'T HOLD OUT LONG ENOUGH. I COULDN'T BE THERE FOR YOU. NOW YOU LIVE IN A SHADOW BOX, BOOK OF PAPER, AND MY SONGS.

VIBE

YOU SPREAD OPEN LIKE A BUTTERFLY
I CRASHED INSIDE AND MATCHED YOUR VIBE

SMOKE A DART IN THE PARK
GET TO KNOWING YOU CLOSER TO MY HEART
I BEAT FASTER AND STRETCH OUT MY EYELIDS
I CAN'T CLOSE MY EYES WHEN I'M AROUND YOU

THE DAYS PASSED OF LIFE LIVED TO FAST
I CRASHED INSIDE AND MATCHED YOUR VIBE

NEVER MISS THE OPPORTUNITY TO LET A WOMAN SHOW YOU HER TRUEST SELF. FOLLOW HER TO YOUR DOOM. FIND SOMETHING YOU LOVE AND LET IT KILL YOU. AT LEAST THE PAIN SMELLS WONDERFUL WHEN INFLICTED BY A WOMAN OF HER OWN PASSION. LET THE TIDE TAKE YOU SOME TIMES. GIGGLE INSIDE AT HOW AMAZING HER STRENGTH IS. HOW LITTLE SHE REALLY NEEDS YOU AND REALIZE YOU ARE WANTED, FOR MAYBE YOUR FIRST TIME. SOMETIMES YOUR LAST. LOVE IT, CHERISH IT, OWN THOSE MOMENTS.

ADAPTIVE ANGER

A PIRATE LIFE
LEFT FROM THE SHORE
NO LAND LEFT FOR HER
A HEART BOUGHT AND SOLD

A HEART OF GLASS
AND A MIND OF STONE
HER LIFE WAS LOST
LONG AGO

GYPSY SALLY NOW
HEART TRADED FOR GOLD
PISTOL GONE IN A GAMBLE
KNIVES AND ROPE LOST HER SOUL

BURIED UNDER SNOW
NEVER TO BE FOUND
HER LIFE WAS LOST
LONG AGO

WOMEN SCOURN WITH GRACE UNKNOWN TO ME. WOMEN TRY AND TRY AND TRY UNTILL THE FATHER LETS THEM BACK IN. THEY UNDERSTAND THE MISSION IN WAYS MEN TRY TO. A MAN IS HERE FOR THE ENDURANCE BUT THE COORDINATION REQUIRED OF A WOMAN IS UNLIKE ANY OTHER CREATURE OF EARTH. IF MAN IS MADE IN GOD'S IMAGE THE FAIRER SEX IS JUST THAT, GOD'S FINAL DRAFT FOR A HUMAN. BEAUTY. BOLD AND UNAPOLOGETIC. COLD AND HEARTLESS WHILE HOLDING MY HEAD IN HER LAP BRUSHING MY CURLS.

CROSSWINDS ABOVE

CROWS MATE FOR LIFE
DRESSED IN ALL BLACK
YOU ARE TRYING TO FLY
BUT MUST BE ALREADY DEAD

THE PAST IN A BLAST
RETURNS RENT FREE
SNORT THOSE MEMORIES
SHAKE TIL THE IMAGE CRACKS

ANGER GETS YOU NOWHERE
EVEN THE SADDEST WORDS
WON'T BRING HER BACK
CROSSWINDS ABOVE

LOST YOU SO MANY TIMES
DECADES AND GENERATIONS
BODIES STACKED WITH LILACS
FERMENT OUR DREAMS

THE BOLD GOTH, PLAYS POSSUM. ADAM AND EVE STARTED A GAME OF CAT AND MOUSE THAT WE WILLINGLY ACCEPT THEN WHEN WE LOSE CRY ABOUT IT. HUMANITY, SOMEDAYS, SEEMS TO BE NOTHING SHORT OF A FOLK SONG. THE SAME OLE STORY TOLD FROM THE CROW'S POINT OF VIEW. NO WONDER THEY CONSUME SOULS IN ANCIENT FOLK LORE. IF REINCARNATION IS REAL THE HOPELESS ROMANTIC IS IN HELL, ALL SEVEN LAYERS AT ONCE.

THE ART, LIFE AND TRIBULATIONS

THE EVENTS AND STORYLINES LEADING INTO
STORIES, POEMS, DRAWINGS, PHOTOS
WHATEVER THE MEDIA, ART IS THE LEAD UP
THE PROJECT, THE ARTIST IS JUST THE VESSEL

LEFT ON THE TABLE NEXT TO THE COUCH
A LOVE LETTER AND FIVE REASONS OF WHY
THE STORY OF WHY WE CAN'T BE TOGETHER
AND HALF A PACKS WORTH IN THE ASHTRAY

MY LIFE PLAYED OUT IN HANDWRITTEN HEARTACHE
NEVER TO BE TOLD MY STORY, JUST TEAR SOAKED
AND NIGHT TREMORS OF MY DEFEAT NO SLEEP
I CAN'T HEAR YOU THERE AFTER TODAY

THE IDIOTS GUIDE TO BECOMING A POET THAT PEOPLE READ, DISCUSS AND TELL ONE ANOTHER ABOUT. ALL THE MOST BEAUTIFUL PHRASES, ALL THE WORDS SET NEXT TO EACH OTHER AND ON TOP OF THE OTHER IN A LEFT TO RIGHT TOP TO BOTTOM MATHEMATICAL PERFECTION OF ART WITH WORDS. JUST TO NEVER GET WHAT YOU WANTED. JUST TO NEVER SEE HER AGAIN. JUST TO FILL ASHTRAYS OF MEMORIES. TO FORMULATE A HANDWRITTEN HEARTACHE. TO BATTLE THE NIGHT TREMORS. SO THAT OTHERS MIGHT BE ENTERTAINED AND MAYBE ONE OF THEM TO TELL YOU, YOU DID GREAT AT SOMETHING. NOTHING.

CACKLE

WHILE THE HYENAS CACKLE ABOUT
THE LION STRETCHES HIS THIGHS

YOU WILL DESERVE AN ENTIRE DAYS REST
YOU MAY NEVER SEE IT THOUGH

LET'S LIGHT THIS CANNON FUSE TO FLAME
AND WATCH THE CARNIVORE ROAR

LIGHT THEM CHERRIES ON FIRE
AND TRY TO BRING ME IN
CAUSE I'M ON THE RUN
WITH A 12 GAUGE SHOTGUN

SLEEP IS THE COUSIN OF DEATH. REST IS NEVER FOR US. DAYDREAM OF BEING FULFILLED AND SKIP THE ACT OF RESETTING. NEVER LOSE AN HOUR THAT TIME ISN'T REAL AND COULD COST YOU WEEKS OR MONTHS OR DECADES. LIGHT YOUR FIRE AND BATTLE ON. A MOVIE "POOLHALL JUNKIES" HAS AN INSPIRATIONAL SPEECH GIVEN FROM CHRISTOPHER WALKEN'S CHARACTER TO THE HERO TOWARDS THE END OF THE MOVIE ABOUT KILLING EVERYTHING IN YOUR DOMAIN THAT DOES NOT RESPECT YOUR MISSION OR COMPLY WITH YOUR PROGRESSION.

ONE WAY

DRIVING DOWN THE ONE WAY HIGHWAY
WITH NO VISUAL OF FIELDS ON EITHER SIDE
JUST ROLLING LINES ONE TO THE NEXT
MIRAGE IMAGE OF YOUR FACE SUBSIDED

THE IRRESPONSIBLE ARTIST TREMBLES ON
NIGHT TERRORS HAUNT THE DAYTIME
FIND A FINE FINALE FOR THE NOISES
CAN'T STOP THE RHYTHM THEY RUN TO

WINTER FALLS UPON THE EARTH AROUND
DOWN THE WINDING GUTTER OF ROADS
HIDDEN WITHIN THE ALLEYWAYS
SHADOW WALKING TO DEFILED TUNES

MANY FALSEHOODS WILL ATTEMPT TO FILL THE VOID OF LOVE. TRUE LOVE. HUMAN TO HUMAN LOVE. GOD'S LOVE IS ABSOLUTE AND OMNIPRESENT. YOU JUST HAVE TO ACCEPT IT'S PRESENCE AND MOVE FORWARD. THE HUMAN LOVE ACCOMPLISHED ON EARTH, TO HELP PROGRESS THE DAYS, THAT CAN BE REPLACED WITH SO MANY TERRIBLE THINGS EVER SINCE THE APPLE. LUST, PORNOGRAPHY. DRUGS, SELF LOATHING. MONEY, CAREERS. EXERCISE AND MEDITATION. ALL GOOD IN MODERATION. SHOULD NEVER GET IN THE WAY OF HAVING A GOOD TIME AND LOVING SOMEBODY. ONE DAY THIS ENDS, IT'S FOR CERTAIN. NEVER MISS THAT CHANCE TO FEEL LOVED AND TO LOVE IN RETURN.

BLUEBERRY

BLUEBERRY FAT AND PLUCKED RIPE
DRIED AND STORED BEHIND GLASS
UNTIL THE DAY A HOLMIE FREES MY BUDDY
BROUGHT YOU HOME AND PUT UPON A SHELF

SET FIRE TO A FRIEND OF MINE
HERE TO LOVE AGAIN
SET ME FREE LITTLE BUDDY OF MINE
WRAPPED IN PAPER OR IN A BOWL

DIESEL SOUR TO THE SENSES
BRIGHT AND DENSE ALL AT ONCE
BROKE OPEN TO BE BURNT AND ENJOYED
FIRE LITTLE BUDDY, SMOKE TO MY LUNGS

BRAIN, BRAIN GO AWAY
FRY AGAIN ANOTHER DAY
WEED SO GREEN ALIVE AND FINE
SMOKE AGAIN EVERYDAY

SWEET LEAF, MARIJUANA. UNTIL THE PHARMACEUTICAL ACT WAS PUT IN PLACE THIS LITTLE LEAF OF JOY AND WONDER HELPED SO MANY. THE RELEGALIZATION OF THIS PLANT MIGHT JUST SAVE HUMANITY. OR AT LEAST CURE A LITTLE BACK AND KNEE PAIN. RELIEVE A LITTLE ANXIETY OR A STOMACH PROBLEM OR TWO. ANYTHING IN MODERATION THOUGH. I DON'T SMOKE BUT MANY BENEFITS HAVE BEEN FOUND IN A SMOKE THAT REPLACES MANY, MANY SYNTHETICS, THAT COULD COST YOU YOUR WATER.

ROOM SERVICE

SWEET LEAFS AND SWEATING IN THE SHEETS
WITH THAT SMOKE IN THE AIR
HOTEL SECURITY BE MAD AT US
BUT WE ORDER ROOM SERVICE ANYWAY

DO NOT DISTURB ON THE DOOR KNOB FOR DAYS
HOT BOXING IN THE BED BLANKETS EVERYWHERE
SMOKE SMOKE AND SMOKE SOME MORE
PURPLE LEAF IN HAND SILK ROPES ON YOUR WRISTS

SLIPPING YOU OUT OF YOUR UNDERWEAR
FOAM PARTY IN THE JACUZZI TUB
NOWHERE IN THE ROOM UNTOUCHABLE
NO WHERE ON YOUR BODY UNEXPLORED

YES, THE HEALING PROPERTIES OF NO RESPONSIBILITIES. A RENTED ROOM WITH A POWERFUL DOOR AND MULTIPLE LOCKS. A VERY COMFY BED. FOOD DELIVERY. A SHOWER JUST STEPS AWAY. FULL CLIMATE CONTROL. A WINDOW HIGH ABOVE SOCIETY THAT WON'T OPEN WIDE ENOUGH TO JUMP OUT OF. CAUSE LIFE MAY NEVER BE BETTER THAN THIS. BUT IT MIGHT SO PUSH ON. DON'T LIVE ANYWHERE FOREVER. LOVE AND EXCESS. PHYSICAL ART. EXPRESSION OF YOU UNTO ANOTHER. ACCEPTANCE OF A LIFE.

SUSTAIN

YOU KEEP LIVING A HALF EFFORT LIFESTYLE
YOU WILL CONTINUE A NON SUSTAINING LIFE

YOU'RE NOT LIVING IN CHAOS
JUST BENEATH YOURSELF
PEOPLE MEANT TO LIVE THE LIFE
FEEL ORGANIC IN IT

THIS FEELS THE WAY YOU DESCRIBE
EVER SINCE YOU MISPLACED YOURSELF

COME AND RUIN MY LIFE
BEFORE I DO

OH, THE CONSEQUENCES OF CHOOSING YOUR OWN LIFESTYLE. THOSE THAT BELIEVE THEIR LIFE IS SO MISERABLE AS TO NEED TO DEVELOP AN ADDICTION THAT WASN'T EVEN GIFTED UNTO THEM FROM BIRTH. THE TRAGIC STORIES THEY SHARE AS A REPLACEMENT FOR HELLO. THE GRAPHIC EVENTS THEY SPILL OUT INSTEAD OF JUST BATTLING THROUGH AND MOVING IN SILENCE.

DEPRESSION IS A FIRST WORLD PLAGUE. ANXIETY IS A MODERN CIVIL WAR. ABORTION AND OVERDOSE THE CURRENT GENOCIDE OF A GENERATION. OVER MEDICATION THE NEW OPEN WORLD INSANE ASYLUM. ELECTRO SHOCK THERAPY IS BIOLOGICAL AND VERY MUCH ALIVE.

PLACID

BEING WHO YOU SAY YOU ARE MUST BE NICE
SO SIMPLE AND EASY DAY TO DAY THE SAME
LUCID AND LANGUID DREAM LAND PLEASANTRIES
STREAMERS FOLLOW MY PUPILS DISLODGED

YOU SEE CLEAR AND CRISP COLORS ACCOUNTABLE
PLACEBO ENTREE DOCILE DOSES DOUBLED DOWN
SUGAR SODA CLEANSE YOUR PALETTE PUTRID
MY MIND NEVER SETTLES LONG ENOUGH FOR SLEEP

SCARE THE DREAMS AWAY WITH REALITY RECOURSE
TERRORIZE THE DECISION MAKER IN MY SOUL
GLOAT ABOUT FROM HIGH UPON YOUR SOAPBOX
TAKE A STAND FOR ABSOLUTELY NOTHING AT ALL

HIGH UPON YOUR SOAPBOX IS WHERE THESE SELF ENLIGHTENED GOVERNORS LIVE. CAREER POLITICIANS ALL THE WAY TO WASHED UP HAS BEENS DESTROYING AN INDUSTRY, CAREER PATH OR HOBBY FROM THEIR COMPLACENT AND ENTITLED STANCE. WHILE POINTING THE FINGER AT ALL THOSE AROUND THEM. DRUNKS AND STORYTELLERS. TELL OF ALL THE WORK THEY DID WHEN THEY WERE YOUNG. ALL THE BIG MOMENTS THEY HAD WHEN THEY WERE YOUR AGE AND STORIES OF THE SUCH. THEY SEE THINGS CLEARER. THEY FIX THINGS BETTER. AND HAVE NO LOGICAL PATH TO ANYTHING GETTING BETTER. THEY REFUSE TO PROGRESS AND WANT YOU TO STAY STAGNANT WITH THEM.

RUNNING FROM THE RAIN

I STEPPED ON A JUNE BUG BUT IT WAS JULY
MY BARE FEET COULD NEVER UNDERSTAND WHY
THE CONCRETE WAS WARMING MY MIND
DENIMS ON MY LEGS WHITE TANK ON MY CHEST

THE CRASH OF THE THUNDER WHEELED ME AROUND
LIGHTNING STRIKES BROUGHT WONDER TO YOUR EYES
DINNER GREW COLD AND I FELT ALONE
YOUR BED NO LONGER INVITES ME IN

I DREW THE KEY FROM MY JACKET POCKET
THE MOTOR FIRED WITHOUT HESITATION NO REMORSE
WHEELS GRABBED ASPHALT THROUGH THE PUDDLES
YOU STAYED BEHIND I DREAMT I'D TAKE ONE WITH

RAIN SOAKED MY SORROWS AND HID MY TEARS
THEY ALL GOT LEFT BEHIND YOU THE FINAL GOODBYE
ALL OF THEM NOT A PHOTO OF FOR THE PRESENT
WE WERE THERE AND NOW THAT'S FINALLY ALL

FRIENDS COME AND FRIENDS GO. WE NEVER NO WHY. WE DO OUR BEST NOT TO INVENTORY OUR ENEMIES THE SAME WAY. THE TRAGEDY FEELS ALWAYS BETTER. THE CONFUSION STAYS CONSTANT THROUGH ALL THE YEARS. WHEN IT'S FRESH AND SOLID WE FOCUS ONLY ON THOSE CLOUDS OF DENSITY TO MATCH OUR CLARITY. WALKING IN THE RAIN OR MEDITATING UNDER A RAIN SPLATTERED AWNING ARE SOME OF MY FAVORITE SETTINGS FOR A STROLE DOWN MEMORY LANE. THROUGH NOSTALGIC NEIGHBORHOODS. JUST TO FIND THOSE PEOPLE THAT GOT LEFT BEHIND. THAT'S ALL.

LOW

LAYING LOW ON LIFE TODAY
JUST TO TRY AND GET RIGHT
KEEPING MY MIND IN THE CLOUDS
TO SLOW THE DARKENING SURROUNDS

THE PAGES FROM THIS BOOK
COMFORT ME IN DEEP WAVES
SOLACE IS ALL AROUND ME NOW
IN MY MIND I WANDER THIS TOWN

MUSIC LULLS THE BACKGROUND
AWAY FLOATS MY INHIBITIONS
LETHARGIC ME CATHARTIC MOOD
I STEEP AND STUMBLE I AM GOOD

WRITING POETRY IS NICE AS YOU CAN REVISIT THE STORIES YOU TELL WITHOUT BURDENING YOUR MEMORY BANK WITH THE STORIES. AS YOU TRY TO LEAVE SLEEPING DOGS LIE. THE MUSIC HELPS TO DULL THE STATIC AND THE SOUNDS I NO LONGER DESIRE. LIKE DRUG ADDICTION IT MOVES ME THROUGH A MOMENT I DON'T WANT. LIFE CAN GET LOW. BUT REALIZE LIFE CAN GET GOOD TOO. LIFE LIVED IN YOUR HEAD WILL NEVER PROVIDE A HEALTHY HARVEST. EVEN IF IT'S NICE TO VISIT FROM TIME TO TIME.

ADOLESCENCE

I ALMOST BELIEVED YOU THIS TIME
IN MY SOBRIETY'S ADOLESCENCE
YOU TREAT ME LIKE A CHILD
WON'T LET ME SEE THE BURN

I'M HERE FOR THE PAIN OF PAIN
WITH NO SUBSTANCE IN THE WAY
I SHOW UP READY FOR THE PLEASURE
I AWAKE I SEE YOUR STRIFE AND I TRY

IN YOUR ATTEMPTS YOU LOST CONTROL
YOU NEVER SHIELDED ME FROM A THING
NOTHING BUT FROM YOUR LOVE, LIFE
STORIES MADE WITHOUT YOUR LOVE

RELATIONSHIPS BASED AROUND AN ADDICTION SOMETIMES GROW BEYOND THE FOUNDATION. BUT I'VE YET TO MEET ONE THAT DID. REVISITING EXES IS ONLY DUMB FOR SUPERFICIAL PEOPLE THAT ARE NEVER CHANGING. IF YOU SURROUND YOURSELF WITH PEOPLE OF CONSTANT GROWTH AND DEVELOPMENT, WHILE YOU YOURSELF ARE A PERSON OF SUCH CHARACTER. THEN REVISITING PEOPLE THAT COME AND GO CAN BE GOOD. BOUNDARIES MUST BE ESTABLISHED AND WALLS GUARDED. IT CAN BE A HEALTHY WAY TO MEASURE YOUR OWN GROWTH AND DEVELOPMENT, THOUGH IT CAN CREATE UNSAFE ENVIRONMENTS. PROCEED WITH CAUTION. IN MY EXPERIENCE SOMEONE NOT WILLING TO OPEN UP, IS NOT WORTH A LOT OF YOUR TIME. SOMEONE WHO OPENS UP TOO MUCH AND TOO SOON. NEEDS RESTRICTIONS AS WELL THOUGH.

FLIGHT PLAN

YOU CAN SMELL THE CALMING GASSES
THEY SCENT THE GOOD ONES FOR REGULATIONS
THE NOXIOUS FUMES DON'T WORK ON US
WE SIT IN IT AND LIVE AS INTENDED BY GOD

IF THERE'S NO CHANCE OF DIEING
WAS THERE A REASON TO AWAKEN
1000 TINY DEATHS CAN'T EXPLAIN
LIFE ON EARTH FOR OUR CALLOUSED HEARTS

I AM THE DRY LOG
COME AND BE MY FIRE
BURNT UP AND ALMOST OUT
LIE UPON ME FOR SUSTENANCE

THE SCENT OF AIRPLANES BOTHER ME MUCH MORE THAN THE "FEAR." THE LIFESTYLE I'VE LIVED AND CONTINUE TO LIVE OUGHT TO DEFEND THE FACT THAT IT'S NOT A FEAR THAT UNSETTLES ME. I HAVE PROVIDED THE WORLD WITH MANY CHANCES TO KILL ME. AIN'T A ONE OF THEM DONE IT YET. NOT THAT I EGG DEATH ON OR TRY TO MOCK DEATH, I JUST DON'T SPEND MY EXISTENCE FOCUSED ON A GUARANTEE. THE OUTCOME OF MY LIFE IS UNKNOWN SAVE FROM THE ONE DAY A VISIT FROM THAT REAPER DRESSED IN A BLACK HOOD. IN THE MEAN TIME I WILL FIND THINGS I ENJOY AND PRACTICE THEM REGULARLY. I WILL DECIDE WHAT MY DAY LOOKS LIKE AND ADAPT AND PROVIDE CONCESSIONS WHEN APPLICABLE. UNTIL THAT DAY.

GONE TOO SOON

WHY DON'T YOU CLIMB UP ON THAT BEER CAN
AND SPEAK RIGHT INTO THE MICROPHONE
FEEL THE RHYTHM FROM THE DRUM LINE
LET THE BASS FLOW THROUGH YOUR HEART

STICK THAT NEEDLE TO YOUR ARM
YOU LOVE TO TELL THEM HOW IT WENT WRONG
YOU FUCKING JUNKIE WE BELIEVED IN YOU
THE PARTY IS OVER NOW, STREET LIGHTS ARE ON

DRIVE A STAKE INTO THE SAND
AND MAKE YOUR CLAIM IN THE DESERT
WATCH THE WIND WASH AWAY
EVERYTHING YOU'VE OWNED

REST IN PEACE

THE IDOLS WE BASE OUR HAPPINESS OFF OF WILL ALWAYS LET US DOWN. THERE IS NO DIFFERENCE IN THE PERSON THAT IS ON STAGE OR IN THE CROWD. JUST THE ACTIONS AND CHOICES. DON'T INVEST TOO MUCH INTO PEOPLE THAT BOOST YOUR ENDORPHINS. DON'T GIVE TOO MUCH GRAVITY TO THE ONES THAT MAKE YOU FEEL SHORT TERM FEELINGS MORE THAN ANOTHER. WHEN THEY SAY TREAT THE JANITOR THE SAME AS THE CEO, THAT HOLDS TRUE ACROSS ALL OF HUMANITY. KEEP YOUR SELF. LOVE YOURSELF AND IDOLIZE YOU BEFORE OTHER HUMANS. BORN ALONE, DIE ALONE. TRY TO ACT LIKE YOU ARE CAPABLE OF SUCH A SIMPLISTIC TASK.

INTERSTATE

I DROVE ALL NIGHT
ON THIS EMPTY INTERSTATE
FULL OF FIENDS AND TRAFFICKERS
THE PUSHERS IN THEIR SHINY CARS

FOR YOU TO NEVER BE HOME
YOU LIVE ALONE IN YOUR
DEPRAVITY
YOU WERE NEVER THERE

NO REASON NO END GAME
EVEN THE STRONG HEARTS FADE
YOU COULDN'T LIVE ALONE
I SEEMED TO FAMILIAR FOR CHANGE

WHEN REVISITING HUMANS OF OUR PAST. THOSE BOUNDARIES MUST BE FIRM AND WALLS GUARDED WITH THE UTMOST INTEGRITY. IF NOT YOU WILL FEEL USED, ABUSED AND HURT BY THE END. AND WE DO IT IN RETURN TO THOSE. REMEMBER PEOPLE ARE VISITING OR REVISITING YOU AS WELL. KNOWING BETTER AND DOING BETTER ARE OPPOSITES.

GRIMY LIFE

SKELETONS ON ALL THE CLOTHES
AWAITING DEATH WHILE SPOUTING
CLAIMS OF NO REASON FOR LIFE
NO PLEDGE ONLY ANARCHY

CIRCLED LETTER A ON SO MANY ARMS
PIERCINGS ALL ABOUT THE FACES
JEWELERS DREAM OF THE SALES
AND LIFE OVER LIVED OVER LOVED

SUBSTANTIAL AND TANGIBLE GOOD
IS FEW AND FAR BETWEEN ANYMORE
A CHICKEN KNOWS NOT OF NUCLEAR WAR
AND I AM TOO SELF AWARE AND SCARED

PUNK ROCK. FREEDOM. THERE WAS A TIME WHERE THOSE TO STATEMENTS WERE SYNONYMS. NOW "PUNKS" PREACH OF THINGS RECOMMENDED BY THE GOVERNMENT. THEY TELL YOU TO AGREE WITH THE MACHINE. BE A COG AND STAY OILED ENOUGH TO WORK BUT DON'T OVER OIL AND SAVE THE COMPANY BEFORE YOU WORRY ABOUT YOURSELF. PACK MENTALITY SERMONS TO PROVIDE FOR THE LEADERS AND SUFFOCATE THE MASSES. PUNK ROCK WOULD'VE BEEN STACKING BODIES BY NOW.

FAME AND UNFORTUNATE

I DON'T NEED TO BE RICH
I CAN SETTLE FOR FAMOUS
I AM THE MAKER OF MY ENDS
I LIVE WITHIN MY MEANS

MY STANDARDS ARE SELF MADE
MY LIFE IS MINE TO DESTROY
MY PAST IS MY EDUCATION
MY FUTURE IS MINE TO FIND

MONETARY GAIN IS MEANINGLESS. THE ARTIST AND RENAISSANCE PEOPLE WE STUDY HAD A HIGH PERCENTAGE OF DIEING POOR. BUT HERE WE ARE SIMPLE LITTLE AFFLUENT HUMANS READING THEIR LIFE STORIES AND WATCHING THEIR DOCUMENTARIES. THEY STUDIED NO ONE AND BECAME LEGENDS. I CREATE WHAT I CREATE THROUGH MY OWN MANIFESTATION. I LIVE WITHIN MY MEANS, DEFINED BY MY OWN SELF STANDARDS. I LIVE AND DESTROY MY OWN LIFE. I LEARN FROM MY MISTAKES AND DEFINE MY OWN LESSONS. ON MY PATH BACK TO GOD'S KINGDOM.

KISS THE VIPER AGAIN

ONE CALL COULD FIX IT ALL
KISS THE VIPER
ONE NIGHT IN THE SKY WITH YOU
KISS THE VIPER
TURNSTILE BLOOD AND VILE
KISS THE VIPER
KISS KISS KISS
THE VIPER

I LOVE WRITING A SHORT POEM AND HAVING A SUPER LONG DEFINITION OF THE WORDS CHOSEN AND THEIR PLACEMENT IN THE PIECE. THIS WON'T BE THAT.ADDICTION; WOMEN, DRUGS, MONEY, EXERCISE, CARS, WORK, ETC. ANYTHING IN MODERATION IS ACCEPTABLE OR DEFENDABLE. EXCESS IS THE MISTAKE.

DEAD INSIDE, DRIVEN

SOBER AND STRIVING FOR SUCCESS
DEAD INSIDE YET INSIDE DRIVEN
DEMEANED BELITTLED BEYOND DOUBT
STILL ON THE SAME TRACK TITLED LIFE

WOMAN LIGHT ME UP LIKE A WATERFALL
SPIT IN MY BEGRIEVED BLOOD AS IT SOURS
AGING QUICKLY WE'RE QUITE ALIKE
NEVER KNEW MIDDLE AGED MAKE IT KNOWN TONIGHT

CALL ME IN, SLEEP OFF YOUR CALLOUSES
I WON'T BE HOME HOLDING YOUR WEIGHT
AEROSOL ARTWORK ON A CONCRETE CANVAS
CALL ME BACK BETRAY ME CARELESSLY

THE END OF CHILDHOOD. THE DEAD WEIGHT BROUGHT ALONG FOR THE JOURNEY. HOARDING THE EMOTIONS THAT ARE LEAST NEEDED FOR THE FUTURE LAID OUT. KNOWING BETTER WE TAKE THEM WITH. SAND DOWN YOUR CALLOUSES AND GROW THEM AGAIN. DON'T FORGET YOUR LESSONS BUT DON'T LET THEM FESTER UNTIL THEY CONTROL YOUR DECISION MAKING. SOME ARE NEVER ALLOWED THE MOMENTS OF OLD AGE. TREASURE EVERY DAY YOU GET BEYOND THE CURRENT. LOVE WOMEN, EVEN IF THEY BRING YOU TO RUINS. THAT WAS YOU THAT FELL, THEY NEVER PUSHED YOU. STAY LOW AND SLOW BUT MOVE FORWARD. DRIVEN AND SCARLESS ARE NOT THE SAME THING SO DON'T ASSOCIATE THEM TOGETHER. SUCCESSFUL PEOPLE ARE NOT SAVED FROM TRAGEDY. THE SAME TRAGEDIES DON'T STOP YOU FROM SUCCESS. 10% SITUATION, 90% YOU. SOME PEOPLE CAN DO A CORNER AT 110. SOME DIE.

DESTINATION

ALOFT

AWAKE, I CAME ALOFT
AMBIENT SCUFFLES AFAR
BEDROOM MEMOIR BEFORE
BURDENS NO MORE

CATER TO CRIES
CARNIVOROUS AND CARNAL
DECADENT AND DEVIANT
DEAD END DREAMERS CAN'T

EVEN FLOW ENDLESS WHISPERS
EVERYWHERE EVERYONE DENIES
FERAL FOREVER AND FREE
FORGOTTEN FEARED FANTASY

GASP AT THE GAP
GIANT RELAPSED GORGED
HEAVY THE HATE
HEROIN OF HEROES LATE

SEX IS NOT THE ENEMY. IT'S AN OFTEN WONDERFUL REPRIEVE FROM SOCIETY. SOMETHING TO BE SHARED THAT PROVIDES A SENSATION AND A CONNECTION BEYOND WHAT YOU CONNECT WITH FRIENDS AND ACQUAINTANCES. MANY MOMENTS CAN BE SAVORED. 1000 TINY DEATHS.TOO MUCH OF A GOOD THING GET'S YOU IN A LOOP. SEE THROUGH THE NIGHTMARES. LIVE. LIFE. LOVE. FOUR LETTER WORDS THAT MEAN A LOT WHEN APPLIED TO THE RIGHT CONVERSATIONS.

MARIVANA

DRUM BRAKES LOCKED UP
POWERING THROUGH IT
WON'T LET A THING IN THIS WORLD
SLOW ME AWAY FROM MY GOALS

GAS TANK GIRLFRIEND
RIDING AWAY NUMBER ONE
EVERY TASK MASTERED
IN MY OWN TIME

MY FIRST THREE EXES
ALL PARTIED LAST NIGHT
HAUNTED MY DREAMS
LEFT ME A FIEND FOR MORE

ALL THE PEOPLE SURROUND US DIEING
MARIVANA
WEED AND ROCK N ROLL GOT ME THROUGH
MARIVANA
NOW SILENCE ON THE SPEAKERS AND YOU
MARIVANA
THEY ALL SAY THE SAME BUT YOUR TOUCH
MARIVANA

THIS SONG KILLED!!! ONE OF THE FIRST SONGS WRITTEN WITH JOHN SAULSBURY ON DRUMS. HEAVIEST, CATCHY JAM FROM 10FOUR10. I LOVE THIS SONG. LYRICALLY, POETICALLY IT'S GREAT. THE RIFF SLAPS. AND THE ENERGY IS RECIPROCATED FROM THE FANS. THE VIDEO ON OUR YOUTUBE CHANNEL IS A BLAST. TO DISECT WHAT'S IN THE CONTENT OF THESE WORDS. VERY SIMPLE. ROCK N ROLL AND THE PARTY LIFE GOT ME THROUGH SO MANY AWKWARD LIFE MOMENTS. SO MANY DEPRESSIONS AND LET DOWNS. STRESSES AND ANXIETIES WERE AVOIDED COMPLETELY. BUT NOW, SOBER. IN LOVE. AND FEELING EVERYTHING. I WRITE MARIVANA. A BUZZ WORD COMBINING MARIJUANA AND NIRVANA. WEED AND ROCK N ROLL. ALL GONE. I LIVE FOR HER VOICE, HER TOUCH. MY GAS TANK GRRLFRIEND. A LOVE SONG. A HAPPY SONG.

CAREFUL MISTER

CAREFUL LIVING DIDN'T GET ME HERE NEXT TO YOU
BUNCH OF MONEY MADE THAT AIN'T OURS
A TOWN FULL OF DEAD FRIENDS IT AIN'T RIGHT
DEAD OR ALIVE I'M COOL AND PLAY THE FOOL

SHADOWS DRESS YOUR FACE
I SHOULD'VE KNOWN THE ANSWER
I WANT SOMETHING AND I'VE BEEN HUNTING
SCOURED THIS EARTH TOO LONG TO NOT KNOW

NOTHING MORE CAME THROUGH
I'LL MAKE YOU A BED IN DREAMLAND WITH ME
CROSS THE DEVIL AND WIN A GAME OF LIFE
MAKE IT AND CALL IT LOVE, KILL AGAIN

LEATHER TOOK THE OIL,
CHAMBER TOOK THE BULLET

THE RETURN OF LOVE. SHE TELLS ME ALL I NEED TO HEAR. LIKE I WAS STUDIED AND RESEARCHED. WHILE I LIVED EACH MOMENT HOPING FOR MY LAST. SHE SAT IN WAITING. DESIGNED TO BALANCE MY ME AGAINST HER. SHE GIVES AND GIVES AND ARGUES BEFORE RECEIVING HER NEEDS. I NEVER UNLOVED HER. I JUST LIVED ON A PLANE THAT SHE COULDN'T EXIST IN. I LIVED THERE FOR EVERYONE ELSE. I LIVED THERE SO I COULD WRITE THESE BOOKS OF POETRY AND RAMBLINGS. THE BABBLES OF AN INTENTIONAL LOSER. HERE BY CHOICE AND SO FORTUNATE SHE CAME BACK AT JUST THE RIGHT TIME.

SUNRISE CIGARETTE

WHAT HAPPENED TO THE DAYS
WE COULD JUST BLAME OUR PAST
SIT BACK GET HIGH AND NEVER MIND
BURN AN ENTIRE DAY ON YOU IN A BED

LIFE WHEN LONELINESS WAS A FEAR
WE KEPT SO MANY DAYS AT WASTE
YOU ME A PILE AND A BOTTLE LEFT
WAY TO A DREARY SUNRISE CIGARETTE

LIFE WOULD FALL AWAY
YOUR SMELL WOULD STAY
AND THE DAY WAS SIMPLE
YOU LOOK BEAUTIFUL
BUT YOU ALREADY
KNEW

AHHH...TO SAY GOODBYE TO ADULTHOOD. TO LIVE THAT PETER PAN FANTASY. LIFE IN NEVERLAND. FREE FOOD. SUSTENANCE IS OUR IMAGINATION. WE PROJECT OUR CHILDHOODS AND LIVE MINIMALISTIC. ONE CONCERN, ONE GOAL FOR THE DAY. NOTHING. AND EVERYTHING THAT FEELS AS CLOSE TO NOTHING. NOW HOOK HAS ARRIVED AND RUINED EVERYTHING. SOME DEAD. SOME INCARCERATED. SOME JUNKIES. SOME IN REHAB. SOME HOMELESS. SOME SUCCEEDING. SOME PARENTING FUTURE FUNCTIONAL MEMBERS OF SOCIETY. SOME DRUNK. SOME WINNING. SOME TYPING THE WORDS YOU'RE READING.

FREEDOM

WHAT I'M DOING IS MY FREEDOM
IN MY HANDS AND WITH MY HEART
TOWELS TIED TO BUCKETS FOR WEIGHTS
CAN'T DROWN YOURSELF IN A SIX OUNCE CUP

FREEDOM CAN WAIT, MY MANTRA NOW
LIVING TODAY JUST DEALING SPADES
ALL THESE SMOOTH EDGES SURROUNDED
EVERYTHING DISINFECTED FOR SAFETY

COUNTING WALLS WITH NO CORNERS TO CUT
BUNCHED UP RAGS TO FLOOD THE FLOOR
EXCITEMENT GROWS STALE IN THE MAIL
I AWAIT MY FREEDOMS FROM WHAT I'VE DONE

THE OVER-INCARCERATION OF OUR GENERATION EATS AT ME. THOUGH I HAVE BEEN FORTUNATE ENOUGH TO KEEP MY ASS OUTSIDE. I HAVE SPENT MANY CONVERSATIONS AND COUNTLESS HOURS AND DAYS WITH PEOPLE THAT HAVE DONE REAL TIME AND SMALL TIME STRETCHES. I WRITE REGULARLY FOR THESE PEOPLE. THE ONE'S I SPEAK OF DIDN'T HAVE A CHANCE. INHERITED DEBT. ADDICTION. MENTAL DISORDER. WRONG PLACE, WRONG TIME. SITUATIONS THAT COULDN'T BE PREVENTED. I KNOW NO GUILTY PEOPLE SAVE 2 OR 3. BUT I KNOW A LOT OF PEOPLE THAT LEARNED HARD LESSONS FOR OTHER'S MISTAKES. OTHER'S MISCONCEPTIONS. LIFE LIVED THAT COULD HAVE BEEN SO FRUITFUL AND SO BOUNTIFUL. BUT SACRIFICED FOR THE RICH AND WRONG. MENTALLY AND PHYSICALLY HOLDING STRONG. A LIFE THAT WOULD HAVE SHOWN A WEAKER SOUL THE BRIGHT SIDE OF SUICIDE. STAY STRONG. STAY SAFE. STAY ALIVE.

DYNAMIC

RASIED BY HYENAS IF I STUMBLE I DIE
IF I FALL IT'S FOR THE LAST TIME
CRY TIL YOUR EYES BLEED SOUR
WATER UNCLEAN FILLS YOUR LUNGS

FRY FRY FRY BEFORE YOU BURN IN HELL
SEVEN LAYERS OF TORMENT, MEET THE VOID
ABSENCE OF LOVE, DISTANCE OF LIFE
A NEVER ENDING PURSUIT OF EMPTINESS

THREE TO FIVE AND TWO MORE YEARS
FOR THE BAD BEHAVIOR IN THE DEATH CAMP
DESOLATE AND SURROUNDED ALONE
ONE IN THE TUBE ON ANOTHER PLAN

PRISON. AND LOCK UP. AN ALL TO RELATABLE METAPHOR. I USE IT IN THIS PIECE TO EXPLAIN LIFE IN THE VOID. LIFE BASED OFF OUR OWN HUMAN AND SIMPLE ACHIEVEMENTS. THE LIMITS OF US. BEFORE A BRAIN LET'S GO AND LET'S THEIR SOUL SPEAK. FOR ME THROUGH THE HOLY SPIRIT UNTO THE HOLY TRINITY. RESPECT OF THE SON AND THE SACRIFICE OF A FATHER. THE LIFE THAT I SAW, I CAN ONLY THANK AND COMPLIMENT FOR IT BROUGHT ME TO MY LORD. I COME OFF BOISTEROUS, LOUD AND CONFIDENT. THAT IS HAPPINESS EMITTING FROM A TORTURED OLD SOUL. THAT IS NOT OF THIS WORLD. FTW.

SHIFTING AND GAMBLING

GRABBING FOR GEARS
LEAVING MY FEARS
GAMBLING WITH HEARTS
RUNNING FROM LIFE AND TIMES

MEMORIES NOIR NOSTALGIA
SHIFTER SLIDING CLUTCH IN
SECOND TO THIRD, CAM HITTING
LAUNCHING IN TO FOURTH

GREASED BACK HAIR
OILED YOUR SILHOUETTE
INK STAINED MY BRAIN
WET SAND MY MIND AWAY

I FIND MANY THINGS ON THIS EARTH TO ENTERTAIN MY MIND. STEAL FROM ME, BEAT ME, ABUSE ME, CALL ME NAMES, JUST DON'T BORE ME. CARS. MOTORCYCLES. ROCK N ROLL. COUNTER CULTURE STUFF. RAT FINK. CLAY SMITH. YOU KNOW COOL STUFF. THE POISONS THAT HAVE SLOWED MY BRAIN SUBSIDE. FAST FOOD. HIGH FRUCTOSE. SYNTHETIC FABRICS. PRESCRIPTIONS. ALCOHOL. PRESERVATIVES. ALL DISAPPEAR FOR MOMENTS OF GOOD. I TRY TO GIVE PRAISE TO THE GOOD EVERY NOW AND THEN.

RUNAWAY DATE

LET'S RUN AWAY AND BE WILD
LIVE IN THE WOODS, FERAL
WITH DIRT BIKES AND A TENT
STEAL FROM THE LOCALS AT NIGHT

IN THE WOODS OF COLORADO
SO WE CAN HOLD UP DISPENSARIES
I'LL BE ARMED TO THE TEETH WITH PISTOLS
YOU CARRY YOUR 20 GAUGE PUMP

CAMPSITE SURROUNDED WITH RAZOR BLADES
STONE DOME KEEPS THE FIRE GLOW LOW
HOMEMADE LEATHER CLOTHES THAT WE
HARDLY USED ON OUR RUNAWAY DATE

I WROTE THIS SONG FOR MY GIRLFRIEND. SHE'S BEAUTIFUL AND STILL FREE. THESE WORDS BRING US SO MUCH JOY. AS SHE PROOF READS MY WORK FOR ME I'M SURE THIS OR MARIVANA WILL BE HER FAVORITE. BUT THIS ONE IS A PROMISED SMILE FROM HER FACE. SHE'S SUCH A HARD WORKER AND SO COMMITTED TO HER LIFE AND HER CHOICES. SHE DESERVES TO BE TAKEN OFF GRID. AND LEFT TO ROAM LIKE A WILD DOG WITHOUT A PACK. I'M NOT CERTAIN HER SPIRIT ANIMAL BUT I DOUBT IT EXISTS ON A PLANE THAT I COULD. SO SHE SACRIFICES AND SHE MAKES CONCESSIONS FOR ME TO KEEP UP WITH HER. SHE IS LOVE. SHE IS A HEELING SOUL AND I AM FORTUNATE FOR HER.

THE SPACE ABOVE THE CLOUDS

SO EUPHORIC AND ENERGETIC
A LIFE UNINHABITABLE BY NATURE
SO CLEAN AND CLEAR EYED
LIKE A HEROINE ON A BEDROOM FLOOR

SO HERE YOU LIVE ABANDONED
NOWHERE TO GET DRUNK AND FIGHT
SO LACKING OF SUSTENANCE
CLEARLY THE BREAD INSUFFICIENT

SO CONVERSATION DISSIPATED
LIFE TAKES MORE THAN THIS
SO COFFEE IS LIFE BLOOD HERE
THE UNKNOWN IS EVIDENT AND UNEASY

SO MANY LOST TO ADDICTION. THEY ARE FREE ONCE WE SAY GOODBYE. LIKE AN OVERDOSE OVER A BREAK UP ON THEIR BEDROOM FLOOR. SO ALONE AND DESPERATE. THEIR EYES GO CLEAR FOR THE FIRST TIME IN SO LONG. BLOOD RUNS FREE. ALCOHOL PICKLES THE LAST ORGAN AND THE BODY STOPS. A SOUL IS SET FREE IN THESE MOMENTS. IF DRUGS COULD DISAPPEAR OR THE REASONS TO USE THEM. THE STRESSES PUT UPON OURSELVES. THE DISBELIEFS WE TELL OURSELVES AND OUR LOVED ONES TO KEEP OUR SICKNESS AT BAY. COMING UP ON 8 YEARS SOBER. I MUST SHARE.

NOT ME

IF I DIE OR FIND A CELL
I WASN'T MEANT TO
BE THERE WITH YOU
TONIGHT WHILE YOU SLEEP

OUT ALONE
FOUND TOO OLD
UNDER A TREE
JUST TAKE A KNEE

IF THE NIGHT WON'T LAST
LET ME LEAVE YOU
A MOCKINGBIRD
TO SING YOU ASLEEP

ROCK ME TO REST
ROLL ME IN A BLANKET
MOSS GROWS OLD
ON MY SKIN I'LL WIN
TONIGHT
TONIGHT
GOOD NIGHT FOR
A LAST TIME

EVERY MOMENT IS A MONUMENT OF A LIFETIME. THEY ALL HAPPEN WITH PURPOSE FOR THOSE OF US TRYING TO ACHIEVE A LIFETIME. THOSE BELIEVING THE HYPE MAY NEVER KNOW. WHAT IT FEELS TO BE TOLD ALL THESE THINGS AGAINST US. AS THOUGH HANDLERS WERE SENT WITH A PASSION WE CAN'T UNDERSTAND JUST TO STOP US. WE CAN'T BUY IN. WE MUST WIN. TONIGHT. OR DIE. TONIGHT. SAY GOOD NIGHT TO ALL SHORTCOMINGS AND ALL FALSEHOODS SHOVED OUR WAY. WIN.

FIND

LET'S FIND OUT THE BOTTOM OF A
BOTTLE IS ALWAYS EMPTY AND DRY
DARE YOU TO FIND PEACE IN YOUR DRUNK

THE SELF AWARE JUNKIE FINDS
NO SOLACE IN SOBRIETY SEES NO
FUTURE IN CHASING A WHITE BUFFALO

THE LAST SEAT AT THE BAR IS SAVED FOR
THE LAST LOSER TO SETTLE INTO TOWN
FIND OUT IF YOU TRY THE EMPTY HIGHWAY

UNLOCK FEATURES IN YOUR BRAIN
NOT MEANT TO BE KNOWN
ACCESS DENIED LONG AGO

IMPLODE UPON REENTRY DIED AND FRIED
ROBOT ARMS DON'T LEAVE FINGERPRINTS

EXCESS WAS DISPROVED DECADES AGO. WE LIVED THROUGH Y2K ALSO. REACH A NEW PLATEAU AND TRY TO SAY HELLO TO A FRIEND FROM BEFORE YOUR MIND WAS UNCOVERED. BEFORE THE INDOCTRINATION TOLD YOU ALL THE THINGS THAT MAKE YOU, YOU ARE WRONG. OPEN UP. KEEP YOUR GUTS. EXOSKELETON OF WIRE MESH. LET YOURSELF BE SEEN. BUT STAY PROTECTED. ABSORB OTHERS, BUT STAY GUARDED. DO BE A JUNKIE. BUT DON'T BE A SQUARE. THERE IS SO MUCH LIFE. WHO TOLD YOU NOT TO LIVE. THIS ENTIRE WORLD IS HERE FOR YOU. AND YOU DON'T HAVE LONG. UNLESS REINCARNATION IS REAL. THEN ADAM AND EVE HAVE TO GET IT RIGHT ONE DAY. DON'T EAT FROM THE SERPENT'S TABLE. KISS THE VIPER GOOD BYE AND GOOD NIGHT.

MAN

RAMEN FOR LUCH
STEAK FOR DINNER
THE MODERN MAN
HIS DIET IS SIMPLE

HIS LOVE IS COMPLEX
LIFESTYLE DISTINCT
YET COMMON DAY
EXPANSIVE AND SYNCHRONIZED

SIN IS AS THE SUN
RISES TO WARM THE DAY
HE NEEDS YOU
LIKE THE SUN NEEDS THE MOON

BEING HUMAN. WELL BEING A MAN, AS IS ALL I CAN SPEAK OF. I'VE NEVER KNOWINGLY BEEN A WOMAN AND DON'T PRETEND TO KNOW THE COMPLEXITIES OF SUCH A LIFE. BUT AS I WAS STATING BEING A HUMAN MAN IS MUCH SIMPLER THAN THEY LEAD US TO BELIEVE. DON'T OVERCOMPLICATE IT. WIN.

APPLE

I'VE NEVER SEEN A MAN
EAT AN APPLE SO ANGRY
AGGRESSIVE GRIP WITH
EACH SIDEWAYS BITE
EYES ON THE CONCOURSE
ALL SEEING
HE LOOKS AT NOTHING
NO ONE HERE FOR HIM

NOT A DROP ESCAPES
HIS CRUSHING JOWLS
HIS LONGING IS EVIDENT
AND EVER PRESENT
THE LOVE IMAGINED
IN THE RED FLESH FRUIT
TO DEVOUR ANOTHER
WOULD NEVER SUFFICE

I REALLY DON'T ENJOY FLYING. IT'S NOT A FEAR. IF AN IN FLIGHT ERROR REALLY OCCURS, IT'S SOMEONE ELSE'S PROBLEM NOW. NOT REALLY A CHANCE OF SURVIVAL FROM THAT HEIGHT. NO WEAPONS ALLOWED AFTER SECURITY. IT'S SAFER THAN PRISON OR WAR. WICH ARE THE MAIN DESTINATIONS SET UPON MY GENERATION BY THOSE BEFORE US. AND BEFORE THEM AND ON AND ON. I HAVE YET TO HAVE A FLIGHT EXPERIENCE THAT I ENJOYED. NO MATTER HOW MUCH I TRY FOR THOSE AROUND ME.

ATMOSPHERE

ATTRACTED TO YOUR ATMOSPHERE
YOUR LOVE WAS LICODE IN A MODERN WORLD
NOW I AM LICOTIC AND AWAITING YOU
TO TELL THE WORLD OF THE LEGEND OF US

THE LOOSELEFT WAS TOO HEAVY
TO BE REAL, SO SURREAL
THE TIL WEIGHED HEAVY
AND YOUR RESUSCITATION BRINGS ME JOY

I DON'T OFTEN SPEAK WITH THE BEST USAGE OF THE ENGLISH LANGUAGE. I SWEAR A LOT IN PERSON AND AM RIDICULED AND SCORNED FOR THAT HABIT. BUT I TRULY DO LOVE THE ENGLISH LANGUAGE. I READ A THESAURUS WHEN I WAS A TEEN. IT WAS GREAT. ONE OF THE FEW BOOKS I'VE READ IN ONE VENTURE COVER TO COVER THAT WASN'T A BIOGRAPHY. PEOPLE FASCINATE ME AS WELL. I HOPE YOU NEEDED A DICTIONARY TO READ THE POEM. I REALLY HOPE YOU READ THE SYNONYMS TO HELP DEFINE THE WORDS. ENGLISH IS NEVER BLACK AND WHITE. SO MANY DEFINITIONS. PRONUNCIATIONS AND MISCONCEPTIONS USING ONLY 26 SYMBOLS. LOVE.

TOGETHER LOVE

THE BUTLER AND THE BAKER
AROSE NEXT TO ME IN A DREAM
I LEFT THE LOCATION WITH FEAR
THE FEAR OF WORKING IN THREES

THE FACADE I MAY BE HANGED
THE ATROCITY OF BECOMING A SERVANT
RUNNING FAR AND MOVING SWIFTLY
I FELL TO A DREAM YET AGAIN

NOW I PLAN TO NEVER SLEEP AGAIN
YOU WERE THERE BUT COULDN'T SPEAK
I REACHED OUT BUT COULDN'T FEEL YOU
TOGETHER LOVE BECAME UNACHIEVABLE

WITHIN A DREAM OF FIRE AND SCREAMS
WITH A LIST OF DEFAMATORY MOMENTS
READ TO ME BY A HOOFED BEAST
FROM INSIDE HIS HOODED REFUGE

I WAS JUDGED AND LEFT A SQUANDER
TO TOIL AND WANDER TO LONG ALONE
IT FELT OF EARTH WITH HUMANENESS
ALL AROUND TIL FOREVER NEVER ENDED

I FEAR REPEATING MYSELF. I HAVE TO STAY OUT OF HELL. I WOULD JUST BE FORCED TO REPEAT MYSELF AND COULD NEVER USE VARIATIONS OF THE ENGLISH LANGUAGE TO SAY THE SAME THING. LITERAL REPEATING. OVER AND OVER AND OVER AND OVER. THE BUTLER AND THE BAKER WAS A CUTE LOVE SHOUT OUT TO MY GRRL. I FEAR LIVING A DREAM WITHOUT GOALS. TO ME THAT'S THE SAME AFORE MENTIONED FEAR. RUN FOR ALL I AM WORTH TO STAY OUT AHEAD OF THESE FEARS. BY ANY MEANS NECESSARY. I DREAM WHEN I AM ASLEEP. DREAMS ARE NOT GOALS AND SLEEP IS CLOSE TO THE END. I DON'T MIND BEING FOUND GUILTY OF MY ACTIONS. BUT CAN NOT ACCEPT A VERDICT OF SOMETHING I AM INNOCENT OF. I WON'T BE SOMEONE'S WINTER.

ASPIRATIONS ANONYMOUS

GREY HAIRED GAS STATION CLERK
ASPIRATIONS ANONYMOUS MEETINGS
THE ALCOHOL WAS NEVER THE PROBLEM
DEAD DREAMS AND CARCASSES OF CURIOSITY

DINED WITH THE DEVIL FOR YEARS
ADDICTION FADED FROM DORMANCY
TWO LANE BLACKTOP TO FLATTOP HAIR
CLEAN YOUR EARS AND SHAVE DAILY

AA. DID GREAT THINGS FOR MY LIFE. I NO LONGER VISIT. THE DUDES THERE ARE TOO MUCH FUN. I HAVE A LOT GOING ON THESE DAYS. MAYBE ONE DAY I WILL BE ALLOWED TO SLOW DOWN AND QUIT MAKING UP FOR MY LOST TIME AND REJOIN THEM GOOD TIME PEOPLE. THE SELFLESS SAINTS THAT RESIDE IN THOSE ROOMS WITH ALL THE LIFE SAVING COFFEE THEY DRINK. ASPIRATIONS ANONYMOUS WAS ALMOST THE TITLE TO MY SHORT STORY. ACT ACCORDINGLY. WAS A CLEANER NAME AND EASIER TO SPELL. THIS POEM WAS TO BE THE INTRO. KEEP YOUR EARS CLEAN AND KEEP YOUR ASS OUTSIDE. LIVE WHILE YOUR NOT PLANTED.

FELL OFF

I ALMOST FELL THE OTHER DAY
THEN I SAT IN A RECLINING CHAIR
LISTENING TO THE PIXIES AND I ATE
CHOCOLATE COVERED CASHEWS
THEN FINALLY THE OLD MILL LOGO
ALL MADE SENSE AND I WAS FINE

I DIDN'T DRINK TODAY
I DIDN'T GET HIGH TODAY
I DIDN'T LOVE TODAY
I DIDN'T WRITE TODAY
I WAS OF ONE MIND AND
DIDN'T FALL OFF TODAY

SOME DAYS, JUST SOBER IS ENOUGH. SOME DAYS ALL I ACCOMPLISH ISN'T ENOUGH. I REALLY NEED TO QUIT MEASURING MY OWN TIMELINES. DAY/NIGHT. ON TIME. EARLY. LATE. 8AM MIDNIGHT NOON 11PM 3 O CLOCK IN THE MORNING. SUNRISE. DUSK TIL DAWN. NONE OF WHICH REALLY MEAN ANYTHING. NOR DID THEY MEAN MUCH. MEDITATION ONLY GOES SO FAR WITHOUT ACTION. AND ACTION IS SO CLOSE TO RELAPSE. SOME DAY IT WILL END. THESE WORDS PUBLISHED WILL BE THERE. THANKS FOR READING ALONG.

ADDICT

ADDICTION IS MOST COMPARABLE
TO A DEVIL WORKING INSIDE OF YOU
FOR THOSE OF US ON THE PILGRIMAGE
ADDICTION JUST WON'T DO
HUNTING FOR HEAVAN HAS ITS TOILS
SHALLOW FACED AND SHALLOW EYES

JUST ENOUGH DEPTH TO DROWN
FACE DOWN IT WON'T TAKE MUCH
YOU CAN EITHER TAKE HEED OR
STOP THE TRAIN WITH SOFT TISSUE
IF YOU STAY YOU'RE MISSING MY ISSUE
WITH YOUR THEORY OF END IT TODAY

LONG EXHALE. I DON'T REMEMBER THE INHALE. THOSE ARE THE GOOD ONES. WHERE GETTING THE OLD OUT IS ALL I CAN FOCUS ON. LIVING A LIFE SHORT OF SUCCESS IS NOT IN MY VOCABULARY. ADDICTS ARE OFTEN MENTALLY OR ARTISTICALLY OR SPIRITUALLY GIFTED. BUT FELL SHORT. AND TRY TO SHUT IT DOWN. YOU WERE MEANT TO LIVE YOUR MEMORIES. DON'T EVER SHORTEN A LIFE YOU DON'T KNOW THE LENGTH OF. KEEP YOUR HEAD UP AND TRUDGE ON WITH US. LIVE YOU. BUT DON'T STOP UNTIL YOU KNOW WHY.

BOTTLE

WHEN THAT BOTTLE STARTS CALLING
BE QUICK TO ANSWER HER SONG
THEY AREN'T JUST CLOUDS PAINTED ON A WALL
THAT'S LIFE HAPPENING IT'S EXISTENCE

THE ONLY THING WEIRDER THAN HER WORDS
WAS HER TASTE IN MUSIC AND ART
SHE SAID WHEN THAT BOTTLE CALLS
DON'T ANSWER ANY MORE

TODAY I HAVE MANY THINGS TO DO
NONE OF WHICH INVOLVE YOU
THE NEXT WEEK ALL HER TIME WAS MINE
I NEVER KNEW A THING ABOUT HER

LET IT BE ME
I'LL DIE IN THAT BOTTLE
IN THAT BOTTLE
BURY ME

A LOVE STORY. PUT TO MUSIC. I AM ACTUALLY AT THE TIME OF WRITING THIS RESPONSE TO BOTTLE. RECORDING THE SINGLE WITH MY FRIEND JOHN ON DRUMS AND MATT BEHIND THE SCREEN. HIS FRIEND CHRIS AND HIM MADE SNAPBACK RECORDS. SUPER HUGE PIVOTAL MOMENT FOR 10FOUR10. GET US OUT PAST "BASEMENT TAPES". AND INTO THE MODERN CENTURY WITH OUR SOUND. BOTTLE IS SOLEMN AND HEART WRENCHING. I LOVED DRINKING. AND THIS DAMNED ART AND MUSIC THING MADE ME SOBER UP. SO I COULD RUN AROUND AND HAVE THE BEST TIME OF MY LIFE FROM A STAGE. SAFELY SINGING BEHIND MY GUITAR. BOTTLE TELLS A STORY I COULD NEVER SPEAK SO I HAD TO SING. I HOPE SHE KNOWS HOW MUCH I MISS HER. NOT JUST THE GOOD TIMES. NOT JUST THE FEELING.

EMPTY HELL

HE WOKE UP IN HELL AMONGST THE FIRE AND FLAME
BUT TO HIS SURPRISE NOT A DEMON TO TAME
HE SEARCHED AND WANDERED TIRELESSLY
FOR THE HELLIONS PROMISED FOR COMPANY

ZERO FOR TEN THE GAMBLER TRIES AGAIN
HE CONTINUES TO FLOW WHILE EMBERS GLOW
PATRICIA HIS LOVE LIVES UP ABOVE
THE LONGINGS TIRE HIS WILL TO INSPIRE

ASPIRATIONS LOST AMONGST THE BARREN LAND
HE AWOKE WITH HIS STRIFE IN HAND
WHY HE SET HIS STANDARDS FOR LIFE
HELL DEVOURED HIS HEART CUTTING LIKE A KNIFE

PATRICIA LONGS TO HIM THROUGH HIS HEART
FEELINGS LIKE THIS THEY READ FROM THE START
TO TELL HER LOVER HER KING THE DEMONS EXIST
AMONGST THE LANDS OF EARTH LIKE A THICK MIST

THE OO GAMBLER COULD NEVER WIN. HE'S A SAFE FRIEND. HE'LL NEVER OUTSHINE OR COMPETE FOR THE SPOTLIGHT. HE LETS ME WIN EVERY TIME. POOR GUY. HE'LL GET HIS ONE DAY. I KEEP PUSHING THE BAND AND PRINTING HIM ON MERCH. HIS MOMENT IN THE SUN WILL SHINE. HE HAS A ROSE ON THE FRONT OF HIS HAT. HE WEARS HIS LOST LOVES OUT FRONT. HIS TEETH HAVE SEVEN ON THE TOP ROW, HE'S A BELIEVER. ONE GOLD TOOTH ON TOP. MONEY OVER ALL. ALL SYMBOLS OF EACH SUIT ON HIS SHIRT. BUT THE SPADE LARGEST, UNTIL DEATH FINDS HIM. THE KING ON HIS SLEEVE, HE IS THE KING OF HIS OWN HEART, HIS OWN WORLD. TWO ZEROS ON THE BACK SIDE OF HIS HAT. HE'S A TWO TIME LOSER AND THAT STAYS WITH HIM. HE WILL WIN.

DIE

WHEN I DIE TELL MY MOMMA IT WAS QUICK
LET HER KNOW I HAD A SMILE WHEN YOU ARRIVED
PORK CHOPS IN THE OVEN MOMMA IT'S ALRIGHT
MY JEANS FITTING JUST RIGHT I LOOK FINE

RIDE THAT MOTORBIKE UNTIL NIGHT FIRE
FLAMES RIDE THE TARMAC IN MY TRAILS
RAMBLE AND SCRAMBLE DREAM ALONG
LEAVE IT ALL AND FIND WHAT MAKES YOU FALL

THE END IS A GUARANTEE.
NOT A THREAT. YOU
SHOULD'VE NEVER SLOWED
DOWN TO APEASE THE FEAR
BESET UPON YOU BY OTHERS.
LIVE WITH THE TENACITY YOU
KNEW AS A CHILD. BEFORE
YOU BECAME A NEAT, WELL
SHAPED COG ON A LARGE
GEAR SYSTEM. IT WILL RUN
JUST FINE WITHOUT YOU.
THERE'S PLENTY OF THOSE
THINGS PRODUCED EVERY
DAY. BUT ONLY ONE YOU.
LIVE LIKE YOU UNDERSTAND
WHAT I JUST SAID. LIVE. WIN.
LOVE.

PENCIL

I PUT A PENCIL TO THIS
AND OUT CAME MY HEART
I KNOW I'M LOVED CAUSE I FIND
AND SHOW THE IMPOSSIBLE IS POSSIBLE
I'M DOING SOMETHING
I DON'T PLAN ON LIVING THROUGH
LIFE ON A RAMPAGE
TO SAVE MY SOUL

IT'S EASIER TO POINT A FINGER THAN
TO LIFT ONE UP TO HELP ANOTHER
BUT I AIN'T DIEING WITHOUT AN
IMPACT ON THE ENTRIE HUMAN RACE

TAKING PICTURES AND
MAKING VIDEOS
ONE DAY I KNOW
YOU'LL BE GONE
I WON'T LIVE THIS TIME
WITH JUST MEMORIES
LOVE LOST ONCE LIVED
DAILY MADE ME CRAZY

I THINK ONE DAY. I'LL ACCIDENTALLY LIVE LONG ENOUGH TO BE A MISSIONARY. I MEAN STAY HERE LONG ENOUGH TO BECOME SELFLESS. TO GIVE UP ON ALL THINGS THAT MAKE ME LEAVE MY NAME ON WALLS AND DRAW ON SIDEWALKS. THAT ALLOWS ME TO LEAVE THE LOVE OF OTHERS WITH ANOTHER. TO BE A VESSEL THAT PASSES GOOD FROM ONE PLACE TO ANOTHER. I WORRY I MAY NOT. I TRY TO SUCCEED AND ARGUE EVERY CHANCE I GET WITH MYSELF AS TO WHAT THAT WORD COULD EVEN MEAN IN THIS DAY AND AGE. WHY I WOULD WANT TO BE A TRAVELING POET AND ARTIST. WHEN PEOPLE ARE KIDNAPPED AND TORTURED AROUND US. WHEN ADDICTION PLAGUES PEOPLE LEFT AND RIGHT. WHEN ABUSE IS SO PREVALENT IT'S COMMON. BUT I CAN'T GIVE UP ON ME TO ACCEPT THE BLEEDINGS OF EVERYONE. WHAT IF MY WORDS CAN HELP. WHAT IF MY MUSIC SLOWS YOUR DAY JUST LONG ENOUGH TO FEEL GOOD. MAYBE I CAN HELP BY LIVING.

ANDY'S SONG(TO HEATHER)

LOVE IN A SCHOOLYARD
WE MET AT THAT PARTY FROM '99
I COULD'VE BURNT MY BOOKS WITH THE FIRE IN MY HEART
STILL GRADUATED FAITHFULLY BY YOUR SIDE

SUMMER LOVE '99
WINTER TIME 2017
I'LL SHOW YOU MY LOVE EVERY CHANCE
TO GROW WITH YOU LIKE A LILLY PEDAL

YOU ROSE UP NEXT TO ME ALWAYS
I AM YOUR HEARTHSTONE THROUGH SICK AND POOR
TO HEALTH AND RICHES IN A HOME FOR OURS
NO DINNER IN ANY RESTAURANT WOULD BE RIGHT WITHOUT YOU

SUMMER LOVE '99
HAPPY 20TH ANNIVERSARY TO MY BEST FRIEND

THE FINAL ENTRY IN THIS YEARS POETRY COMPILATION WROTE ITSELF. I WAS COMMISSIONED BY MY FRIEND ANDY HINTZ TO WRITE AN ANNIVERSARY SONG FOR HIS WIFE. THE CONTENT HE SHARED WITH ME, I MEAN IT, WROTE ITSELF. I WAS HONORED TO BE APART OF THEIR STORY. I AM SUPER PLEASED TO END ON A HIGH NOTE. THEIR LOVE SONG.

ONLINE RESOURCES

*MERCH, MUSIC AND LITERATURE AVAILABLE AT

WWW.10FOUR10.BANDCAMP.COM

*FOLLOW THE MUSIC

WWW.FACEBOOK.COM/10FOUR10

*ENJOY THE MUSIC

YT CHANNEL: @10FOUR10

STREAM* 10FOUR10 *TODAY

TikTok and InstaGram - joe10four10